# The Invisible Man

H. G. Wells

# ABOUT YOUR BOOK

| | |
|---|---|
| **▶ MP3** | Go to Helbling e-zone to listen to or download the activity |
| 🎧 | Listen to the story |
| 💬 | Talk about the story |
| glossary• | When you see the blue dot, check the word in the glossary |
| **P** | Prepare for Cambridge English Exams: B1 Preliminary |
| **FACT FILE** | Read informative fact files which develop themes from the story |
| **LIFE SKILLS** | Make comparisons between the story and contemporary life |
| **e·zone** | Go to Helbling e-zone to do activities |

# FOR THE TEACHER

A state-of-the-art interactive learning environment with 1000s of free online self-correcting activities for your chosen readers.

Go to our Readers Resource site for information on using readers and downloadable Resource Sheets, photocopiable Worksheets and Answer Keys. Plus free sample tracks from the story.
**helbling.com/english**

For lots of great ideas on using Graded Readers consult Reading Matters, the Teacher's Guide to using Helbling Readers.

# Contents

# HELBLING DIGITAL

## INTERACTIVE ONLINE TEACHING AND LEARNING MATERIALS

**THE EDUCATIONAL PLATFORM**

**HELBLING e-zone is an inspiring new state-of-the-art, easy-to-use interactive learning environment.**

Use the **personal access code** on the inside front cover of this book to unlock a host of self-correcting activities, including:

- reading comprehension;
- listening comprehension;
- vocabulary;
- grammar;
- exam preparation.

**TEACHERS** register free of charge to set up classes and assign individual and class homework sets. Results are provided automatically once the deadline has been reached and detailed reports on performance are available at a click.

**STUDENTS** test their language skills in a stimulating interactive environment. All activities can be attempted as many times as necessary and full results and feedback are given as soon as the deadline has been reached. Single student access is also available.

1000s of free online interactive activities now available for **HELBLING READERS** and your other favourite Helbling Languages publications.

**ONLINE ACTIVITIES**
## helbling-ezone.com

## helbling.com/readersblog

**Love reading and readers and can't wait to get your class interested? Have a class library and reading programme but not sure how to take it a step further? The Helbling Readers BLOG is the place for you.**

The **Helbling Readers BLOG** will provide you with ideas on setting up and running a Book Club and tips on reading lessons **every week**.

- Book Club
- Worksheets
- Lesson Plans

**Subscribe** to our **BLOG** and you will never miss out on our updates.

# ABOUT THE AUTHOR

**Herbert George Wells** (or H. G. Wells) is considered, along with the French writer Jules Verne, to be the father of science fiction•. He was born in Bromley, near London, in 1880, to a modest family. When he was eight, he broke his leg and was confined to• bed for a long time. His father brought him books from the local library and he became a keen• reader.

Due to his family's economic situation, Wells could not go to school, but he read and studied on his own. He became so proficient• that a school offered him the position of student-teacher. This meant that he was able pay for his own education by teaching younger pupils. He then went to Imperial College in London to study biology, and graduated in zoology at the University of London.

His novels have been hugely popular since their publication, and some of them have become films. He invented themes that became classic in science fiction. He also predicted technological developments that became reality, like space travel. A crater• on the dark side of the Moon is named after him. Some of his stories are very realistic: Orson Welles' radio adaptation of his novel *The War of the Worlds* convinced people that an invasion• from Mars was really happening in New Jersey. He also wrote about social justice• and human rights•.

H. G. Wells died in London in 1946, probably from a heart attack.

- **confined to:** had to stay in
- **crater:** hole in a planet, moon or star made by a comet
- **human rights:** basic rights every person should have
- **invasion:** (of an army) attempt to take control of an area by force
- **keen:** (here) very interested
- **proficient:** very good at something
- **science fiction:** stories about life in the future on other planets
- **social justice:** concept that all people should have equal rights to wealth, justice, health, etc.

# ABOUT THE BOOK

Today many people enjoy stories about time travel, invasions by strange beings from other planets, etc. But in 1895, when H. G. Wells published his first novel, *The Time Machine*, about a journey to the future, readers knew only two genres• in fiction. One was realism, i.e. fiction about the real world (past or present), and the second was fantasy, i.e. fiction about impossible worlds, creatures and events. H. G. Wells (and Jules Verne), like the scientists in their stories, invented a new genre: science fiction. Science fiction is based on future developments in science and technology. *The Time Machine* was an instant success.

The late nineteenth century was a time of technological discoveries. These discoveries were suddenly changing society and the way people lived, and the changes were happening very quickly. New questions needed answers: what will be the effect• of technology on society? Are scientists going too far? And above all: if something is technologically possible, should we automatically create it? Is there a danger that evil• people will gain control• of the new technology and use it to their advantage? In science fiction, writers and readers are able to explore their feelings about whether scientific advances are always good for people and the planet.

**The Invisible Man**, published in 1897, was H. G. Well's second science fiction novel. It starts with the arrival of a mysterious stranger in a small village in southern England during a snow storm, and explores some difficult questions about scientific inventions.

- **effect:** change or result that is caused by something
- **evil:** very cruel
- **gain control:** take control or power away from somebody else
- **genres:** types or styles of books, films, etc.

7

# FROM HORROR TO SCIENCE FICTION:
## MARY SHELLEY'S
# FRANKENSTEIN

What happens when science goes beyond nature? This is one of the main themes of *The Invisible Man*. However, it was not the first time that this theme appeared in literature. It is also at the heart of Mary Shelley's *Frankenstein*, first published in 1818.

In this novel, Victor Frankenstein, a brilliant young scientist builds a body using parts of corpses• and then brings it to life. However, the 'Creature' (as he is called in the book) is a monster• and Frankenstein rejects him. The Creature runs away and discovers that his appearance terrifies people. In his anger against his 'father', he kills Victor's youngest brother. He is very lonely and begs Victor for a female companion.

When Victor refuses, the Creature kills Victor's wife and also his best friend. In the end the experiment• destroys both the creator and the creation. *Frankenstein* raises important questions about the relationship between science and ethics•. This is why the most famous horror story of all time is also a precursor• of science fiction. The tragedy occurs because Victor is unable to deal with the terrible results of his experiment. He does the experiment because he is obsessed•, without thinking of the possible consequences•. Victor tries to protect the people he loves, but fails. He knows he was the real cause of their deaths and feels huge guilt.

- **consequences:** results of an action (usually bad)
- **corpses:** dead bodies
- **ethics:** ideas about what is right or wrong for society
- **experiment:** scientific test to discover if something is true
- **isolation:** the state of being away from other people
- **monster:** creature that is ugly and frightening
- **obsessed:** thinking about one thing all the time
- **outcast:** someone rejected from a society or group
- **precursor:** something that comes before another similar thing

It is Victor's inability to manage the results of his experiment that makes the Creature a real monster. At first the Creature hides in the woods and secretly helps a poor family that lives nearby. He tries to be part of society: he learns to speak by listening to the family, then he finds some books and teaches himself to read and write. But when he tries to connect with the family, they reject him in fear, and he becomes desperate. He understands that without Victor's help, he will always be an outcast•. He asks for a companion, but Victor will not create one because he believes the Creature is bad. He fears that if he gives the Creature a wife, they will bring an evil race into the world. Victor's refusal means that the Creature must live a life of total isolation•, so he decides to make Victor's life desperate and lonely, too. The story is a true tragedy.

CARL LAEMMLE
presents

"FRANKENSTEIN"
THE MAN WHO MADE A MONSTER

A UNIVERSAL
PICTURE

What happens when human intelligence produces a monster? And who is really the monster? What happens when a human makes a scientific discovery and uses it in a monstrous way? These are some of the questions *Frankenstein* and *The Invisible Man* raised. The world is still discussing them today.

# WHAT ARE YOU LOOKING AT?

**Article 12 of the Universal Declaration of Human Rights•** says that everyone has the right to the protection of the law against interference with their privacy or attacks on their privacy. This includes their family, home, correspondence and also their reputation•.

## SURVEILLANCE• SOCIETY

An old legend tells the story of a man who knew what other people were thinking. He could read other people's minds and was unhappy as a result. He was lonely because nobody knew him the way he knew everybody else. One day he met another man who could read other people's minds. They instantly hated each other.

This is a reflection on the idea that we all want someone who understands us completely, but we also need privacy•. We need to be free to choose who has information about us and what they know about us. We need people to trust us even if they don't know everything about us. We feel uncomfortable when we know people are watching us. We need some 'invisibility'. These are some of the reasons why privacy is a basic human right.

- **CCTV:** closed-circuit television; cameras in public places that film everything that happens there
- **logged:** recorded
- **personal data:** information about people and their lives
- **privacy:** space alone without other people seeing or hearing
- **reputation:** what people think about you
- **store:** keep for use in the future
- **The Universal Declaration of Human Rights** is an international document that was adopted by the United Nations General Assembly on 10 December 1948. It states the basic human rights of all human beings.

# SO HOW MUCH PRIVACY DO YOU HAVE TODAY?

## CCTV•
Every time you go into a shop, public building and many private buildings, and when you move through the streets of your town or city, you are filmed by CCTV cameras.

## SOCIAL MEDIA
If you have a social media account, you probably use it to share a lot of private information about yourself: your photos, where you are, what you are thinking, who you are with, what you are doing, other people's posts, who you follow and everything you 'like' or react to. Your personal data• and all these activities are recorded and sold to data analysts. They produce a secret profile that describes you. How did you set your privacy settings? Can people you don't know see your page? Who can see your data? What do they do with your data? Who can see your secret profile? Do you know what that profile says about you?

## YOUR MOBILE PHONE
You are probably terrified by the thought of losing your mobile phone, because so much of your 'life' is in it. However, how private is all that life you store• in your phone? Your location, every text message, every phone call, every app you use and every website you visit are logged•. Do you know what happens to these logs? Do you know who can access them?

Which of these types of surveillance are acceptable to you? Why? Which of them are not? Why?

Mr Hall

Mrs Hall

Dr Kemp

Colonel Adye

The Invisible Man

12

# The Invisible Man

Teddy frey

Mr Bunting

Mr Jaffers

Mr Thomas Marvel

13

# BEFORE READING

**1** **Match the jobs to the descriptions of what the characters do.**

> **1** policeman   **2** scientist   **3** doctor   **4** landlady
> **5** tramp   **6** chief of police   **7** vicar

**a** ☐ Dr Kemp studies and researches science.

**b** ☐ Mrs Hall is the owner of an inn.

**c** ☐ Mr Bunting is a priest in the Church of England.

**d** ☐ Mr Cuss looks after people who are ill.

**e** ☐ Mr Jaffers is called when someone breaks the law.

**f** ☐ Colonel Adye is in charge of all policemen in the village.

**g** ☐ Mr Marvel has no home, job or money; he lives on charity.

**2** **Read the two character descriptions from the story. Which characters from Exercise 1 are they describing?**

**a** .................. had a large face, a big nose, a wide mouth and a strange beard. He was fat, with short arms and legs. He wore a very old silk hat, and his coat had shoelaces instead of buttons. He was sitting by the roadside, not far from Iping.

**b** It was early evening and .................., a tall and slender young man, was sitting in his study on the hill overlooking Port Burdock, doing some important scientific research.

**3** **Find the two place names in Exercise 2. Then find out which part of England they are in. Are they both real places?**

**4** **Look at the pictures. Match the two sentence halves below. Then write the names under the pictures.**

........................   ........................   ........................

........................   ........................   ........................

........................

| | | | | |
|---|---|---|---|---|
| **a** | ☐ | We use test tubes | **1** | and cover a window. |
| **b** | ☐ | Goggles are glasses | **2** | that protect the eyes. |
| **c** | ☐ | Shutters look like little doors | **3** | to cut trees and wood. |
| **d** | ☐ | Handcuffs are put | **4** | to stir a fire. |
| **e** | ☐ | A poker is used | **5** | and carries things. |
| **f** | ☐ | We use an axe | **6** | on a person's wrists. |
| **g** | ☐ | A cart is pulled by a horse | **7** | in scientific experiments. |

# BEFORE READING

**1** **Look at the diagrams and read the sentences. Then complete the sentences using the words in bold.**

A glass is transparent and **refracts** light.
A mirror **reflects** light.
A banana **absorbs** most light, but **reflects** yellow light.

**a** If an object ........................... light, the light goes into the object but doesn't go through it.
**b** If an object ........................... light, the light goes through but it changes angle as soon as it enters the object.
**c** If an object ........................... light, the light hits the object and bounces from it.

**2** **Read the extracts from *The Invisible Man*. Answer the questions.**

It was great. I felt like a man who could see in a city of the blind. But soon I realised that there were problems. I could avoid people coming towards me, but not people behind me. And crowds were dangerous for me.

I began to see the problems. I had no shelter and no clothes. If I wore the clothes, I lost all my advantage.

**a** Why were people behind the Invisible Man a problem?
**b** Why were crowds dangerous for him?
**c** Why did the Invisible Man lose his advantage if he wore clothes?

**3** 💬 **Work with a partner. Can you think of other disadvantages of being invisible? What advantages are there?**

**4  Read the text and match the words in bold to their definitions.**

Negative feelings can be difficult to manage, and different people respond differently. When something unexpected happens, people are surprised. If the surprise is great, they may take in air quickly, in other words, they may **gasp**. If it is an unpleasant surprise, people can be **startled**, and they will react in different ways. For example, a child may **stamp** their feet on the ground to express frustration and **exasperation**. Adults who are normally calm may become anxious and **distressed.** Others can become impatient and **irritable**, get angry at small things and **lose their temper** easily. When people are angry, some express it in private by **punching** things like pillows, but others can become **aggressive**. If they lose control, they can start **raving** about the situation or **smashing** things. It is very important to learn to recognise negative feelings when they start, so you can deal with them in a healthy way.

a  ........................... : breaking something noisily, usually glass
b  ........................... : annoyance about something you can do nothing about
c  ........................... : hitting with one's fist
d  ........................... : surprised, especially by something negative
e  ........................... : in an angry and violent way
f  ........................... : take a short, quick breath through the mouth because of surprise or pain
g  ........................... : lose control and become angry suddenly
h  ........................... : put one's foot down on the ground hard and noisily
i  ........................... : very upset and worried
j  ........................... : speaking in an uncontrolled way because you are angry (or ill)
k  ........................... : easily annoyed

**5  What do you think will happen in the story? Do you think the novel will have a happy ending?**

# 1 THE STRANGE MAN'S ARRIVAL

The stranger• came to Iping on the 29th of February, through a cold wind and snow storm, walking from Bramblehurst railway station with a large suitcase. He was wrapped up• from head to foot, with big blue goggles•, a scarf and a hat that together hid every bit of his face except the tip of his nose. There was snow on his shoulders and chest. He staggered• into the Coach and Horses more dead than alive and dropped his suitcase.

'A fire,' he cried, 'Please! A room and a fire!'

He followed Mrs Hall, the landlady•, into the guest sitting room. She lit the fire and went into the kitchen. She started cooking the bacon, then went back into the sitting room to lay the table. Although the fire was burning nicely, she was surprised to see that the stranger was still wrapped up.

'Can I take your hat and coat, sir?' she said, 'and give them a good dry in the kitchen?'

'No,' he said looking out of the window. 'I prefer to keep them on.'

'Very well, sir,' she said. 'In a bit the room will be warmer.'

He didn't answer. Mrs Hall laid the table quickly and left the room. When she returned, he was still standing there. She put down the eggs and bacon noisily, and said loudly, 'Your lunch is served, sir.'

'Thank you,' he said, and did not move.

- **goggles:**
- **landlady:** (here) woman who owns a pub or an inn

- **staggered:** walked unsteadily
- **stranger:** person who is not known in a particular place
- **wrapped up:** covered with clothes

19

When Mrs Hall went back, she knocked and entered without waiting for an answer. The stranger was sitting at the table and moved quickly to pick something up from the floor. She noticed his coat and hat on a chair in front of the fire. She looked at them and said, 'May I take them to dry now?'

'Leave the hat,' said her visitor, in a muffled• voice. She turned and for a moment she was too surprised to speak.

He was still wearing his gloves and he was holding a white cloth• over the lower part of his face. That was the reason for his muffled voice, but it was not what startled• Mrs Hall. It was the fact that all of his head above his blue goggles, including his ears, was covered by a white bandage•. The only visible part of his face was his pink nose. He was still wearing his scarf, and strands• of thick black hair were coming out between the bandages.

She put the hat back on the chair. 'I didn't know, sir...' she began.

'Thank you,' he said.

'I'll have it dried, sir,' she said, and took his coat and left.

'The poor man has had an accident• or an operation that disfigured• him,' thought Mrs Hall as she put his coat in front of the kitchen fire.

## MRS HALL
Why does Mrs Hall think the stranger has had an accident?

- **accident:** unexpected event that hurts someone
- **bandage:**
- **cloth:** piece of material used for clothes

- **disfigured:** changed his appearance in an unpleasant way
- **muffled:** unclear and quiet
- **startled:** surprised
- **strands:** long pieces

20

When she cleared away the stranger's lunch, he said that his luggage was at Bramblehurst station.

'Can I have it sent here?' he asked. Mrs Hall said a cart• could go there the next day.

'Not earlier?'

Mrs Hall saw the opportunity to find out the reason for her guest's appearance. 'It's a steep• road, sir,' she said. 'A cart lost control there about a year ago. Two men died. Accidents, sir, happen in a moment, don't they?'

'They do.'

'But people take a long time to get well again, don't they? My sister's son, Tom, cut his arm at work, and he was bandaged for three months. My sister had to do his bandages, and then undo them. So if you don't mind, sir, could I ask…'

He interrupted her. 'Will you get me some matches? My pipe• is out.'

His rudeness• upset Mrs Hall. She stared• at him for a moment, then she went for the matches.

'Thanks,' he said, turning his back to her to look out of the window.

'He's very sensitive on the topic of accidents and bandages,' thought Mrs Hall. But his rudeness irritated her. He remained in the sitting room for the rest of the day.

## THE STRANGER

What is unusual about the stranger?

Why do you think the stranger is rude?

If someone is rude to you, what do you do or say?

💬 Tell a partner.

- **cart:** Kutsche
- **pipe:** Pfeife

- **rudeness:** way of behaving that is not polite Unhöflichkeit
- **stared:** looked directly Starren
- **steep:** (of a hill) that goes up or down very quickly

# 2 MR TEDDY HENFREY'S FIRST IMPRESSIONS•

At four o'clock, Mrs Hall was trying to find the courage to go in and offer her visitor some tea. The man who repaired clocks, Teddy Henfrey, came into the bar, so she asked him to check the old clock in the sitting room.

She knocked on the door. When she entered, she saw her visitor asleep in the armchair, with his bandaged head on one side. The only light in the room was from the fire, which lit his goggles but left his face in darkness. For a second, she thought that he had an enormous mouth that filled the lower half of his face. Then he woke up and put his gloved hand over his mouth.

She brought the lamp in and saw him more clearly. He was holding the white cloth to his face, so she couldn't see his mouth. 'Well,' she thought, 'it was probably just a shadow.'

'Would you mind, sir, if this man looks at the clock?' she asked.

'Go ahead,' he said.

Mr Henfrey came in, but when he saw the stranger, he stopped suddenly.

The stranger greeted him, and then spoke to Mrs Hall. 'Have you made any arrangements about my luggage at Bramblehurst?' he asked.

'I have,' said Mrs Hall. 'The postman will bring it tomorrow morning.'

'Thank you', said the stranger. 'I was too cold and tired earlier to explain that I am a scientist. My luggage contains my equipment. I like to be alone when I do my research•, so please don't disturb• me. I had an accident and my eyes sometimes hurt so much that I have to be in the dark for hours. When that happens, the smallest interruption• is very upsetting. Is this clear?'

'Certainly, sir,' said Mrs Hall, and left the room.

---

- **disturb:** stop or interrupt someone when they are busy
- **first impressions:** first idea or opinion about someone or something
- **interruption:** moment when one action stops another
- **research:** work to discover facts

Mr Henfrey started to work very slowly, hoping to discover more about the stranger.

'The weather...' Mr Henfrey began.

'Why don't you finish and go?' said the stranger, clearly irritated. 'It's not a complicated job.'

'Certainly, sir,' Mr Henfrey finished and left, but he was very upset. In the village he met Mrs Hall's husband, and he told him all about the stranger.

'Looks like a disguise•, doesn't it?' said Mr Henfrey. 'He's taken your rooms and he hasn't given a name. And he's got a lot of luggage coming tomorrow. He says it's equipment, but who knows? It could be anything.'

## RESEARCH

What does the stranger say about his work and how he works?
Do you believe him?
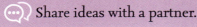 Share ideas with a partner.

---

• **disguise:** change of appearance to hide one's identity

# 3 THE THOUSAND AND ONE BOTTLES

The next day the postman brought the stranger's luggage on his cart. Mr Hall was outside the inn, waiting to bring the luggage in and playing with the postman's dog.

The stranger came out wrapped up as usual. As soon as the postman's dog saw him, it began to growl angrily. Before the postman could stop it, the dog bit the stranger and tore his glove and trouser leg. The stranger rushed back into the inn and went up to his bedroom.

'I'd better go and see if he's all right,' said Mr Hall. He went upstairs and since the stranger's door was open, he walked in.

The room was dark. All he saw was a handless arm, then he was struck• violently• in the chest• and thrown out of the room. The door was slammed• in his face and locked•.

He stood there in shock and then went outside.

After a moment the dog began growling again.

'Hurry!' shouted an angry voice in the doorway. There stood the stranger, fully covered, with a different pair of gloves and trousers.

'Were you hurt, sir?' said the postman. 'I'm really sorry, the dog...'

'Not a bit,' said the stranger. 'Bring my boxes in.'

As the boxes were carried into the sitting room, the stranger unpacked them quickly. They contained hundreds of test tubes• and bottles with powders and liquids of all colours, some labelled Poison. And as soon as the boxes were unpacked, he started to work.

- **chest:** front part of a person's body between the neck and stomach
- **locked:** closed with a key
- **slammed:** shut with force and noise
- **struck:** hit
- **test tubes:**
- **violently:** with force

When Mrs Hall took his dinner to him, he was so absorbed in his work that he did not hear her until she put the food on the table. Then he half-turned his head and immediately turned it away again. But she saw he wasn't wearing his goggles, and his eye sockets• seemed strangely empty.

## EMPTY

What is the title of this novel?
What does 'invisible' mean?
What things make us think that the stranger may be invisible?
What would you feel and think if you were Mr and Mrs Hall?

He put on his goggles again, and then turned towards her. 'Please don't come in without knocking,' he said in the exasperated• tone that was now normal for him.

'I knocked, but you...'

'Perhaps you did. But in my research — my very urgent and necessary research — the slightest interruption... I must ask you...'

He was so strange and aggressive• that Mrs Hall felt scared. But she was also losing her patience• with him.

'Certainly, sir. You can lock the door, you know. Any time.'

'Yes,' said the stranger. He turned and sat down with his back to her.

All afternoon he worked with the door locked. Once Mrs Hall heard a bang• and the sound of bottles ringing together, and she went to listen outside his door.

'I can't go on,' he was raving•. 'It's too much! It may take me all my life! Fool! Fool!'

And then all was silent again.

- **aggressive:** behaving in an angry and violent way
- **bang:** loud noise
- **eye sockets:** holes for eyeballs in one's head
- **exasperated:** annoyed and frustrated
- **losing (her) patience:** becoming annoyed with someone's behaviour
- **raving:** speaking in an uncontrolled way

# 4 THE BURGLARY• AT THE VICARAGE•

Not much happened until Whit Monday•. The stranger spent all his time working in the sitting room and had no communication with the world outside the village. Most of the time he was extremely irritable•, and once or twice things were broken with sudden violence. He often talked to himself. Mrs Hall listened carefully, but she never understood what she heard. The children called him names and everybody disliked him.

The burglary at the vicarage happened on Whit Monday. Mrs Bunting, the vicar's wife, woke up suddenly before dawn, with the strange feeling that somebody was in the house. She heard the sound of bare• feet, and she woke her husband as quietly as possible. In the dark, Mr Bunting put on his glasses and went out on the landing• to listen. He heard noises in his study downstairs, and then a violent sneeze•.

He picked up the most obvious weapon, a poker•, and went down the stairs as noiselessly as he could. Mrs Bunting followed him.

The house was dark and quiet. Then something broke and there was the sound of rustling paper. They heard someone swearing•, then a match was struck and the study was filled with yellow light. Mr and Mrs Bunting were now in the hall. Through the open door they could see the desk with a drawer open and a candle burning on the desk. But they could not see the burglar.

- **bare:** (here) without shoes  *barfuß*
- **burglary:** act of entering a building and stealing something  *Poltergeist*
- **irritable:** easily annoyed
- **landing:** area in a house at the top of the stairs
- **poker:**
- **sneeze:** when air comes out of one's nose and mouth uncontrollably  *niesen*
- **swearing:** saying rude words  *fluchen*
- **vicarage:** house where a vicar lives
- **Whit Monday:** religious holiday

They heard the sound of rustling paper again — it was the savings• the vicar kept in the drawer. Holding the poker firmly, Mr Bunting rushed• into the room, closely followed by Mrs Bunting.

'Hands up!' he cried•, and then stopped amazed — the room was completely empty.

For half a minute, perhaps, Mr and Mrs Bunting stood with their mouths open, then they looked everywhere. They couldn't find anybody, but the money was gone.

There was a violent sneeze in the kitchen. As they rushed into the kitchen, they saw the back door open. Nobody went in or out, but the door closed with a slam.

## THE BURGLARY

Who is the burglar?

Have you or someone you know had a burglary?

What happened?

Tell a partner.

- **cried:** spoke loudly  schreien
- **rushed:** moved quickly  huschen

- **savings:** money kept aside for the future
  Geldversteck

## 5 THE FURNITURE THAT WENT MAD•

The same day, Mr and Mrs Hall got up very early. As he was going down the stairs, Mr Hall noticed that the stranger's door was open. Then when he got downstairs he saw that the front door was not locked. He remembered locking it the night before. He went upstairs and knocked on the stranger's door, then pushed the door open and entered.

The room was empty and their guest's clothes and bandages were scattered• on the bed. He called his wife, who was downstairs.

'He's not in his room,' he said, 'but his clothes are. What's he doing without his clothes? And the front door is unlocked.'

They thought they heard the front door open and shut, and someone sneezed on the stairs. Mr Hall thought it was his wife downstairs. She thought it was her husband upstairs.

As Mrs Hall joined her husband in the stranger's bedroom, an extraordinary thing happened. The stranger's clothes gathered themselves together and jumped onto the floor. Then the hat flew straight at Mrs Hall's face. And the chair rose in the air with its four legs pointed at Mrs Hall and flew towards her. She screamed• and turned away. The chair legs came gently but firmly against her back and forced her and Mr Hall out of the room. The door slammed violently and was locked and then suddenly everything was quiet.

Mrs Hall almost fainted• on the landing.

- **fainted:** passed out; lost consciousness
- **scattered:** thrown in an untidy way
- **screamed:** shouted in a high voice
- **went mad:** (here) went out of control

'It was spirits•!' said Mrs Hall. 'Don't let him come in again. I knew he was bad — he put the spirits into my furniture!'

They called the neighbours and told them what happened, and soon a small crowd gathered downstairs, discussing what to do.

Suddenly, upstairs the stranger's door opened. As they looked up in amazement, they saw the fully covered figure staring at them with those blue goggles. He came down the stairs slowly, then he entered the sitting room and slammed the door in their faces.

## GO MAD

'Mad' has two different meanings. What are they?

What is the chapter title?

How did the furniture go mad?

• **spirits:** ghosts

# 6 THE UNVEILING° OF THE STRANGER

The stranger remained in the sitting room until about midday. People heard him walking up and down, smashing° bottles and shouting. He rang the bell three times furiously°, but no one answered him.

Then the news of the burglary at the vicarage came, and people put two and two together°. Mr Hall and a neighbour went to the police station.

It was a beautiful day, and outside people were getting ready for the village fair°. Inside the inn, the little group of scared but curious people increased. Suddenly, the stranger opened his door and stood staring at the people in the bar.

'Mrs Hall!' he called.

Mrs Hall appeared, holding a little tray with an unpaid bill on it.

'Do you want your bill, sir?' she said.

'Why haven't you prepared my meals and answered the bell?'

'Why isn't my bill paid?' said Mrs Hall.

'I told you three days ago I was waiting for a postal payment…'

'I told you two days ago I wasn't going to wait for any postal payments. You're five days late.'

'I told you that my payment hasn't come. Still, I've found some money…'

'I wonder where you found it,' said Mrs Hall.

That seemed to annoy the stranger very much. 'What do you mean?' he asked.

- **furiously:** in a very angry way
- **put two and two together:** understood the cause of a situation
- **smashing:** breaking something noisily, usually glass
- **unveiling:** showing something publicly for the first time
- **village fair:** event in a village with stalls and entertainment

'That I wonder where you found it,' said Mrs Hall. 'And before I take any bills or get any breakfasts, you have to tell me one or two things. I want to know...'

Suddenly the stranger raised his gloved fists• and stamped his foot•. 'Stop!' he shouted with such violence that he silenced her instantly.

'You don't understand,' he said, 'who I am or what I am. I'll show you.'

He put his open hand over his face and then he moved it. The centre of his face became a black hole.

'Here,' he said, and gave Mrs Hall something. She held out her hand automatically, but when she saw what she was holding, she screamed loudly and dropped it suddenly. The stranger's nose, pink and shining, was on the floor.

Then he removed his goggles, and everyone in the bar gasped•. Then he took off his hat and his bandages. 'Oh, my God!' said someone.

## PREDICT

What has happened? Explain in two or three sentences.

What do you think will happen now?

Make some predictions.

Then read the rest of the chapter.

Were you right?

- **fists:**
- **gasped:** took a short, quick breath through the mouth because of surprise or pain
- **stamped (his) foot:** put his foot down on the ground hard and noisily

Mrs Hall screamed and ran to the door. Everyone ran out. They were prepared for scars•, disfigurements, visible horrors, but *nothing*! Everyone fell on everyone else, because the man who stood there shouting an incomprehensible• explanation had no head.

Everyone in the street ran towards the inn. A crowd quickly gathered and started talking about the headless stranger. They were looking into the inn to try and see him. Mr Hall and Mr Jaffers, the village policeman, arrived. They went into the sitting room and saw the headless figure, who had bread in one gloved hand and cheese in the other.

'What do you want?' said the stranger.

'Head or no head, mister,' said Mr Jaffers, 'I'm here to arrest you.'

A fight followed, during which the stranger's gloves also came off, and more people joined in.

'Stop! I surrender!•' cried the stranger. He stood up breathing heavily, headless and handless. 'The fact is, I'm all here — head, hands and everything, but I'm invisible. I know it's strange, but it's not a crime. Why do you want to arrest me?'

'The reason why I'm arresting you,' said Jaffers, 'is not invisibility — it's burglary.'

'I'll come,' said the stranger, 'but no handcuffs•.'

'I'm sorry, sir, but the rules...' said Jaffers.

Suddenly the figure sat down, and the shoes, socks and trousers came off.

---

- **handcuffs:** metal circles that the police put on someone's wrists when they arrest them

- **incomprehensible:** impossible to understand
- **scars:** marks on the skin left after an accident
- **surrender:** stop fighting and admit defeat

'Stop that!' said Jaffers, realising what was happening. He tried to hold on to the stranger's coat, but it was soon empty in his hand.

'Hold him!' shouted Jaffers. 'If he gets the shirt off...'

The shirt-sleeve punched• Mr Hall's face, and the next minute the shirt was on the floor.

'Hold him!' said everyone, and they all started hitting everybody else, moving towards the door and then down the steps of the inn. In the street a woman screamed as something pushed her. A dog was kicked and ran away howling•, and with that, the Invisible Man left Iping.

## HOLD HIM!

How could you stop the Invisible Man?
Think of ways with a friend.
Share them in class.

---

• **howling:** (of dogs or wolves) making a crying sound

• **punched:** hit with fist

# 7 MR THOMAS MARVEL

Mr Thomas Marvel had a large face, a big nose, a wide mouth and a strange beard. He was fat, with short arms and legs. He wore a very old silk hat, and his coat had shoelaces instead of buttons.

He was sitting with his feet in a ditch• by the roadside, not far from Iping. He was looking at his old boots and trying on another pair. He didn't know which pair to choose.

'They're just boots,' said a Voice.

Marvel looked over his shoulder to reply, but he was amazed to see no one there. He stood up and looked around. Still no one.

'Where *are* you?' he said. 'What's going on?'

'Don't be afraid,' said the Voice.

'Where *are* you?' said Marvel. 'Are you *dead*?'

He was suddenly taken by the neck and shaken violently.

'It's very simple,' said the Voice. 'I'm an invisible man.'

'What?' said Marvel.

A hand gripped• his wrist and made him jump. His fingers touched the hand, went slowly up the arm, and found a bearded face.

'Incredible!' he said. 'Invisible — except…'

He looked at the empty space more closely. 'Have you eaten bread and cheese?' he asked.

---

- **ditch:** long narrow hole next to a road for water to pass through
- **gripped:** held tightly

'I have, and my body hasn't completely digested• them yet. Listen, I need help. I was desperate, and then I saw you and I thought, "He's an outcast• like me." I want you to help me get clothes and shelter• and some other things.'

'Oh, I don't know,' said Marvel. 'This is all too strange for me.'

'I've chosen you,' said the Voice. 'Help me, and I will do great things for you. An invisible man is a man of power. But if you betray• me, if you don't do as I say…' He paused and hit Marvel's shoulder.

Marvel cried in terror at the touch. 'I don't want to betray you,' he said. 'I'll help you — just tell me what I have to do.'

## MARVEL

What do we learn about Marvel's life?

What does the Invisible Man want him to do?

💬 Talk with a partner.

- **betray:** behave in a dishonest and disloyal way
- **digested:** (here) absorbed
- **outcast:** someone rejected from a society or group
- **shelter:** temporary protection from danger or bad weather

# 8 MR MARVEL'S VISIT TO IPING

 People were enjoying the Whit Monday village fair when Marvel entered Iping. Nobody knew him, but several people noticed him.

From inside his shop opposite the Coach and Horses, Mr Huxter saw him go into the inn and then come out a few minutes later. Marvel looked around and walked towards the gates of the yard•. He stopped at the gate, filled a pipe and started to smoke. Suddenly he put his pipe in his pocket and went into the yard. He reappeared with a big bundle• in a blue tablecloth in one hand and three books tied together in the other.

'Stop thief!' cried Huxter.

Marvel began to run and Huxter set off after him. But after only a few steps he tripped up• for no reason and fell face down.

In order to understand what happened, we need to go inside the inn. When Mr Huxter first saw Marvel, Mr Cuss, the village doctor, and Mr Bunting, the vicar, were in the guest sitting room of the Coach and Horses. They were looking at three big books full of incomprehensible symbols and numbers when the door suddenly opened.

- **bundle:**
- **tripped up:** fell over something
- **yard:** area outside a house

A stranger walked in. 'Is this the bar?' he asked.

'No,' said both gentlemen at once.

'Over the other side,' said Mr Bunting.

'Please shut that door,' said Mr Cuss.

'All right,' said the stranger, in a completely different voice.

Then he spoke in his first voice and said, 'Fine. Door closing!' and closed the door.

As the two men sat down to examine the books, they each felt a hand on their necks.

'Where did you learn to read a scientist's private diaries?' said a Voice. The men's heads were banged on the table at the same time.

'Where are my clothes?' The two heads hit the table again.

'Listen,' said the Voice. 'I could kill you both and get away quite easily if you don't do what I ask. I want clothes and those three books.'

## REASONS

Discuss the questions with a partner and give reasons for your answers.

What do you think is in the bundle?

Who is the stranger?

Why does the Voice want the books?

# 9 THE INVISIBLE MAN LOSES HIS TEMPER•

While these things were going on in the sitting room, and while Mr Huxter was watching Marvel smoking his pipe, Mr Hall and Mr Henfrey were in the bar next door. They heard a loud noise, a cry, and then silence.

'Something's wrong,' said Mr Hall and knocked on the door.

'Are you all right there?' he asked.

The conversation stopped suddenly, and then started again. Mrs Hall arrived, and the two men were telling her about the first noise when there was another noise.

'Sh!' said Mr Henfrey. 'Wasn't that the window?'

Everyone was standing outside the sitting room listening intently when Mr Huxter appeared in the street, shouting 'Stop thief!' At the same time a loud noise came from the sitting room, followed by the sound of windows being closed.

Everyone in the bar rushed out into the street. They saw someone running round the corner holding a parcel, and Mr Huxter flying through the air and landing on his face. Mr Hall and two customers started running after the thief. But after just a few yards, Mr Hall screamed and also went flying, taking one of the customers to the ground with him. The second customer tripped up like all the others.

More people from the village came running round the corner. At first they stopped, astonished to see the lane• empty except for the three men on the ground. When they started running again, one by one they fell on top of each other.

---

- **lane:** narrow road
- **loses (his) temper:** loses control and become angry suddenly

43

Mr Cuss came out of the inn wearing a white sheet round his waist•. 'Hold him! He's got my trousers! And all of the Vicar's clothes!' he shouted and fell face down on the street.

The village was full of people running and doors slamming, and after a few minutes it was deserted. For two hours nobody found the courage to go out into the street.

Meanwhile•, Marvel was walking along the road to Bramblehurst, carrying the three books and the big bundle.

'If you try to run away again,' said the Voice, 'I will kill you.'

## TEMPERS

What kind of things do people do when they lose their temper?

Look at the chapter title. How does the Invisible Man lose his temper?

Do you ever lose your temper?

Talk with a partner.

• **meanwhile:** during the same period of time

• **waist:**

# 10 THE MAN WHO WAS RUNNING

It was early evening and Dr Kemp, a tall and slender young man, was sitting in his study on the hill overlooking Port Burdock, doing some important scientific research. As he looked out of the window, he saw a short man in a very old hat running down the hill towards the town.

'Another fool who believes the stories in the newspapers and runs around shouting "The Invisible Man is coming!"' Dr Kemp thought with contempt•.

But in Port Burdock, those who saw the terror on Marvel's sweaty face didn't feel contempt. They stopped and stared up and down the road with worried faces. And then something — a wind, a sound like heavy breathing• — rushed by.

People screamed, jumped off the pavement, ran into their houses and slammed their doors. 'The Invisible Man's coming!' they shouted.

Inside the Jolly Cricketers pub at the bottom of the hill, the landlord•, a cab driver, an American man and an off-duty• policeman were talking.

'What's the shouting about?' asked the cab driver.

There was the sound of someone running heavily and the door was pushed open violently. Marvel, weeping• and dishevelled•, rushed in.

'He's coming!' he screamed in terror. 'The Invisible Man! Help! Help!'

'Who's coming? What's going on?' said the policeman, and went to lock the door.

'Help me!' cried Marvel, staggering and weeping, but still gripping the books. 'Lock me in somewhere. I ran away. He's going to kill me!'

'You're safe,' said the American. 'The door's shut. What's it all about?'

---

- **breathing:** taking in and letting out air from one's lungs
- **dishevelled:** very untidy
- **landlord:** (here) man who owns a pub or an inn
- **off-duty:** not at work
- **weeping:** crying
- **with contempt:** without respect for someone or something

A blow• suddenly shook the door.

'Hello,' cried the policeman, 'who's there?'

The landlord helped Marvel hide behind the bar. A window was smashed in, and outside there were sounds of screaming and running. Then everything was quiet.

'Let's unlock the door,' said the American, and showed them a small gun. 'If he comes in, I'll shoot• his legs.'

He unlocked the door and took a few steps back.

'Come in,' he said.

## MARVEL

What has happened to Marvel so far?

In pairs make a list.

The door remained closed.

'Are all the other doors locked?' asked Marvel.

'Oh, no!' said the landlord. 'The back door!'

He rushed out of the bar and he reappeared after a minute.

'The back door was open!' he said. 'He may be inside now!'

- **blow:** (here) sudden loud hit against something
- **shoot:** fire a bullet from a gun

Suddenly there was a terrible noise, then a scream, and Marvel was dragged towards the kitchen. The policeman and the cab driver rushed after him. They managed to get hold of the Invisible Man, but they were punched and kicked. However, Marvel ran away, and the men in the kitchen found they were fighting with air.

'Where has the Invisible Man gone?' cried the American. 'Outside?'

'This way,' said the policeman, going outside.

Stones• started to fly towards the men.

'I'll show him!' shouted the American and shot five bullets• in the direction of the stones.

A silence• followed.

'Get a light,' said the policeman. 'Let's try to find his body.'

## VIOLENCE

What violent things does the Invisible Man do and say in this chapter?

Think of other violent things he has done or said.

Then look back through the book and check.

• **bullets:**

• **stones:**

• **silence:** period of no sound

# 11 DOCTOR KEMP'S VISITOR

 Dr Kemp heard the shots•.

About an hour later, the doorbell rang. The servant• answered, but she didn't come upstairs to announce a visitor, so he called her. 'Was that a letter?' he asked.

'It was just someone who rang the bell and ran away, sir,' she said.

At two o'clock that night Dr Kemp stopped working and went downstairs to his bedroom. As he crossed the hall, he noticed a dark spot on the floor. He touched it — it looked like drying blood•. Then he went to his bedroom, but he stopped astonished: there was blood on the handle of his bedroom door.

He went in and heard something moving in the room. Suddenly, he saw a bandage with blood on it, hanging in mid-air. He stared at this in amazement. The bandage was tied around something, but it seemed empty. He tried to touch it, but his hand met invisible fingers. He recoiled• at the touch and his face went white.

He looked at the bed. There was blood all over it and the sheets were torn. Then he thought he heard a low voice say, 'Kemp!' But Dr Kemp did not believe in voices.

'Stay calm, Kemp. I need help.'

'This is impossible,' said Kemp. 'It's a trick.' The hand gripped Kemp's arm, and the two men fought, but the Invisible Man was stronger and threw Kemp on the floor.

- **blood:** see illustration
- **servant:** someone who works and lives in a house doing cooking, cleaning, etc.
- **shots:** bullets fired from a gun
- **recoiled:** moved back in fear

'If you shout, I'll smash your face,' the Voice said. 'This is no magic. I really am invisible. And I want your help. It's amazing to find you here, Kemp, just by chance. I'm Griffin, of University College. Do you remember me? Medicine student, younger than you, almost an albino•, tall, with a pink and white face and red eyes. And I have made myself invisible.'

'How can a man become invisible?' said Kemp.

'I'm sorry about the blood — it gets visible as it coagulates•. Only living tissue• can be invisible. I'm starving and cold. Have you got a dressing gown• to lend me?'

Kemp gave Griffin his dressing gown and some food. Then he watched the gown take shape and sit on the chair. He asked Griffin about the shooting, but the man was exhausted• and didn't make much sense•. He talked about Marvel with long silences between his words.

'That tramp has stolen my books and my money. I could see he wanted to run away… Why didn't I kill him!'

'Where did you get the money?' asked Kemp.

'I've had no sleep for nearly three days,' said the Invisible Man. 'I'm sorry, but I can't tell you tonight. I really must sleep. Don't tell anyone I'm here. Or else…'

'I won't. You can have my room.'

The Invisible Man checked all the doors and windows to make sure he could escape if he needed to. Then Kemp heard him yawn•.

## KEMP

What is the connection between the Invisible Man and Kemp?

- **albino:** person or animal with no pigment/ colour in their hair, skin and eyes
- **coagulates:** changes from liquid to semi-solid
- **didn't make sense:** was hard to understand
- **dressing gown:**

- **exhausted:** very tired
- **tissue:** material that animals and plants are made from
- **yawn:** breathe in deeply from one's mouth due to tiredness or boredom

50

# 12 CERTAIN FIRST PRINCIPLES•

Kemp couldn't sleep. He went into his study and found the day's newspapers. He read all the articles about the events in Iping, but none of them mentioned a tramp.

'He's not only invisible,' he thought, 'but he's mad! Murderous•!'

Kemp was still awake at dawn, trying to believe the unbelievable. He told the servants to prepare breakfast for two in the study, and then to stay in the kitchen. The morning papers arrived and he read about the events at the Jolly Cricketers and a man called Marvel, but there was little information and no mention of the books.

'He's angry,' he thought, 'and dangerous… The things he might do! And he's here… What should I do?'

He went to his desk and wrote a note. He addressed the envelope to *Colonel Adye, Port Burdock* and gave it to his servant to deliver.

Just then Griffin woke up in a bad temper. Kemp heard him smash something in the bedroom, so he went to knock on the door.

'What's the matter?' he asked.

'Nothing,' was the answer.

They had breakfast in the study.

'Before we can do anything else, I must understand more about this invisibility,' said Kemp, watching food disappear above the headless, handless dressing gown.

'Well,' said Griffin, 'after London, I moved to Chesilstowe. I left medicine and took up physics to study light. Light fascinated• me. An object absorbs• light or it reflects• or refracts• it, or does all these things. If it doesn't reflect or refract or absorb light, then it cannot be visible.'

---

- **absorbs:** takes in
- **fascinated:** very much interested
- **first principles:** fundamental concepts that scientific theories are based on
- **murderous:** capable of murder; dangerous
- **reflects:** sends back (doesn't take in)
- **refracts:** changes the direction of

'I know,' said Kemp, 'But I still don't understand how...'

'I discovered a formula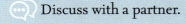 for invisibility. It is possible to make a substance refract light in the same way as air does. It then becomes invisible. It's all in the books that tramp has stolen.'

Kemp listened in amazement.

'I discovered that it's possible to bleach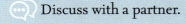 blood and keep all its normal functions. I could also make a living tissue transparent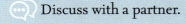. All except the pigment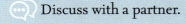. And then I realised what this knowledge meant for me, an albino — I could make myself invisible! But after three years of experiments, I found that I couldn't complete my project.'

'Why not?'

'I didn't have enough money,' said Griffin. 'So I robbed my father. The money wasn't his, and he shot himself.'

## ALBINO

Find the sentence with the word 'albino' in it.
What is an albino?
Why does the Invisible Man want to make himself invisible?
Does this change your feelings about him?
Discuss with a partner.

---

- **bleach:** cause material to become white with chemicals or light
- **formula:** method for achieving something
- **pigment:** natural colouring of living tissue
- **robbed:** stole from
- **transparent:** you can see through it

# 13 THE HOUSE IN GREAT PORTLAND STREET

They sat in silence, then Griffin continued his story.

'I moved to London. I rented a large room in a big lodging house• in Great Portland Street. I used my father's money to buy the equipment I needed and I built my machine. I worked day and night. The work was nearly finished when my father killed himself. That was last December. I went to the funeral• because I had to, but I didn't feel sorry for him – all I could think of was my research.'

Kemp listened in silence.

'In my first experiment I put some white wool fabric in my machine. It was the strangest thing in the world to watch the wool fade• and disappear. I couldn't believe it myself, but I touched it and it was there. Then I heard a meow behind me, and saw a white cat outside the window.'

'And you made her invisible?

'I made her invisible. I bleached her blood, and I gave her chloroform•. Then I bandaged her and put her in the machine. She woke while she was still a mist•, and meowed loudly and horribly. The old woman from downstairs knocked on the door. Her white cat was all she had. I gave the cat some more chloroform and answered the door. "Did I hear a cat?" she asked. "A cat? Not here," I said, very politely, and I sent her away.'

## FEELINGS
Who didn't the Invisible Man feel sorry for? Why not?
Who or what do you feel sorry for in this chapter? Why?
What do you think will happen next? Make a prediction.

- **chloroform:** chemical that can make people unconscious
- **fade:** slowly disappear
- **funeral:** church service after someone dies
- **lodging house:** house with rooms to rent
- **mist:** tiny water drops in the air

'How long did it take?' asked Kemp.

'Three or four hours. The bones, the tendons• and the fat were the last to go. But the coloured part in the back of the eyes didn't go. So when she woke up, she was like a ghost — just two eyes moving. She started meowing, very loudly, and of course she was impossible to catch. So I opened the window and finally the meowing moved outside.'

'Go on,' said Kemp.

'The next day the landlord knocked on my door. He said he knew I spent my nights vivisecting• cats and wanted to look at my machine. He wanted to know if I was doing something illegal or dangerous. I lost my temper. I pushed him out, slammed the door and locked it. But this was a problem.'

'Why?' asked Kemp.

'I didn't have enough money to move to another house. Invisibility was the only solution. So I took my books and my money and put them in a locker• at a post office. Then I made myself invisible.'

'Did it hurt?'

'Yes. It was unimaginably painful, but that didn't stop me. I watched my body become like glass, and then the bones, veins and arteries faded. The tendons disappeared last. In the end, I was exhausted. I slept all morning, with my face covered because the light came through my eyelids.'

- **locker:** small cupboard that can be locked
- **tendons:** tissue that attaches muscle to bone
- **vivisecting:** using animals in scientific experiments

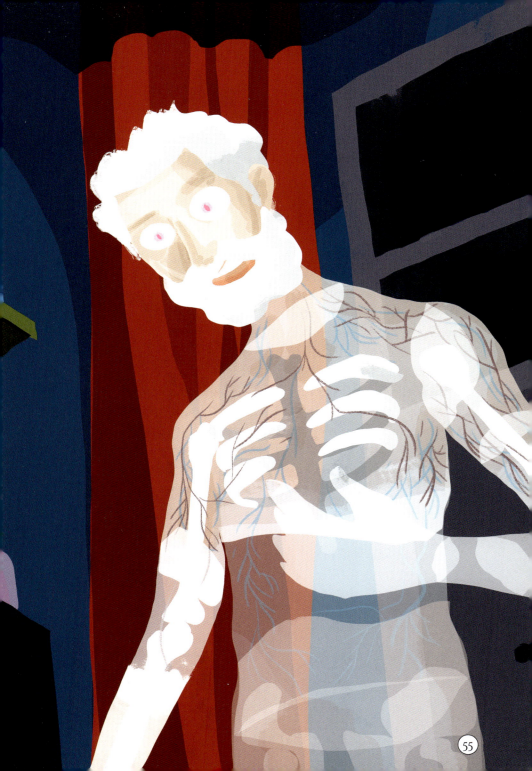

'And then what happened?'

'At about midday the landlord knocked on my door. Very quietly I put the parts of my machine in different places around the room, so that nobody could put it back together. He opened the door and entered with his two sons and the old woman from downstairs. They were amazed to find the room empty. They checked every corner and under the bed, and they were disappointed to find no "horrors". When they left, I quietly put all my papers, the bedding and the chair in the middle of the room. Then I lit a fire with some matches, and left.'

'You set the house on fire!' exclaimed• Kemp.

'It was the only way to cover my tracks•. I left quietly and went out into the street. I was invisible. I started planning all the things I could now do with no fear of punishment•. It was great. I felt like a man who could see in a city of the blind. But soon I realised there were problems. I could avoid people coming towards me, but not people behind me. And crowds were dangerous for me.'

'Ah! If people can't see you, they'll think there's nothing there…'

'Exactly. I started walking in the gutter•. It hurt my feet because it was rougher than the pavement and I had to keep jumping out of the way of the traffic. And, without clothes, I was very cold, because it was January, and the mud• on the road was freezing. Then I discovered that dogs could smell me. I had to run when one started chasing me and barking.'

---

- **cover (my) tracks:** hide evidence (of my presence)
- **exclaimed:** said in a surprised way
- **gutter:** the edge of the road, where rain and water flow
- **mud:** brown substance which is a mixture of earth and water
- **punishment:** act of doing something bad to someone because they did something wrong

'What an impossible situation!'

'I ran for a while before I realised that the road was too crowded. I couldn't go back because of the dog. So I ran up the steps of a house and stood there waiting. The dog turned around and ran away.'

'Go on,' said Kemp.

'Then two boys stopped near me. "Can you see them?" said one. "See what?" said the other. "Those footprints• of bare feet." I looked down and saw they were looking at my footprints on the white steps. "A barefooted man went up those steps and didn't come down," said one. "And his foot was bleeding•." And then he pointed at my feet, and I realised that splashes of mud showed the shape of my feet. "Look!" he said. "It's like the ghost of a foot!" and he moved to touch my feet.'

'What did you do?'

'I stamped my foot. The boy jumped back in surprise and I jumped onto the steps of the next house. But the other boy followed the movement. He started shouting, "Feet! Look! Feet running!" I ran and ran until my feet got hot and dry and stopped leaving footprints.'

## PROBLEMS

What problems does the Invisible Man have now that he is invisible?
Would you like to be invisible?
Talk with a partner.

---

- **bleeding:** releasing blood

- **footprints:** marks that you leave with your feet if you walk in the snow or with dirty or wet feet

# 14 THE HOUSE IN DRURY LANE

'I was tired, hungry, miserable, cold and in pain, and then I realised that a snow storm was approaching! Suddenly I had an idea. I went to Omniums, the big store where you can buy everything, from food to paintings. I found a quiet area in an upper floor and I hid, waiting for closing time. When the cleaners left, I was alone in the huge store. I took all the clothes I needed, some money and food. Then I went to sleep in the beds department.'

'Go on,' said Kemp.

'I woke up suddenly and saw two shop assistants approaching. They saw me and they started chasing me. I got away a few times and then the police arrived. I realised that the only way I could get out of there was by being invisible. So I took my clothes off and left. I began to realise the problem. I had no shelter and no clothes. If I wore clothes, I lost all my advantage•. Even eating was impossible, because before the food is fully digested, it's visible.'

'I never thought of that,' said Kemp.

'Nor had I. And there were other dangers. Snow, rain, fog and dust make my outline visible — I wasn't going to remain invisible for long. Then I remembered that there are shops that sell theatrical costumes•.'

'Good idea!' said Kemp.

---

- **lost (my) advantage:** was no longer in a better position
- **theatrical costumes:** clothes worn by actors

'I found an old-fashioned, dark theatrical shop, with a dark house above it, in Drury Lane. There was no one inside and I entered. As I opened the door, a bell rang. So I left the door open and hid, waiting for someone to turn up. A short, thin man, hunched•, with thick, dark eyebrows, long arms and very short bandy• legs came through the back door. "Those boys again!" he said. He closed the front door and went to the back door. I moved to follow him but he heard me and stopped. He went out of the back door quickly and slammed it in my face.'

'Why did you want to go into the house?' asked Kemp.

'Because there was nothing I could use in the shop, and I hoped he had more in the house. He came back to check the shop and he left the door open, so I went inside. I found myself in a little room with another closed door to the house upstairs. I waited until he came back and opened the door. Then I slipped• behind him as he went upstairs. He stopped suddenly, listening, and I very nearly walked into him.'

'That man's hearing was incredible!' said Kemp.

'It was. He kept going in and out of rooms, slamming the doors before I could follow him. The house was very old, with rats everywhere. I managed to get into a room full of clothes, but he heard me and came in holding a small gun. He looked around, walked out and locked the door. I made a noise to make him come back, and when he did, I knocked him on the head with a chair. Then I gagged• him and tied him up•.'

- **bandy:** that were wider at the knees than the thighs or ankles
- **gagged:** put something in someone's mouth to stop them speaking
- **hunched:** with shoulders and back bent forward
- **slipped:** (here) moved quickly
- **tied (him) up:** tied rope around someone to stop them moving

'You left him tied up?'

'I had to. Then I searched the whole house, and I found what I needed —
a false nose, goggles, a wig, clothes and shoes. I also found some money.  I
checked myself in a mirror — I looked strange, of course, but not impossible.
So I walked out into the street, and no one seemed to notice me.'

'What happened next?', asked Kemp, glancing out of the window.

'Well, I realised that I couldn't eat in public without revealing my invisible
face. And when I thought about it more, Kemp, I realised it was stupid and
crazy to be an Invisible Man. I thought about all the things most people
want. It's true that invisibility made it possible to get them — but it also
made it impossible to enjoy them.'

'But why did you go to Iping?' said Kemp, anxious to keep Griffin talking.

'I went there to work. To find a way of undoing my invisibility, after I
have done everything I plan to do.  And that is what I want to talk to you
about now.'

## REALISATION

What important thing does the Invisible Man realise?
What reasons does he give?
What does he want now?
How do you feel about him? Say why.

- **wig:** false hair you can put on your head

# 15 THE PLAN THAT FAILED•

Kemp glanced• out of the window and saw three men approaching the house. He stood up so that Griffin couldn't see them.

'So what's your plan now?' he asked.

'I need to get my books from that tramp. Do you know where he is?'

'He's in the town police station, by his own request,' said Kemp, a little nervously, hearing footsteps outside.

'My mistake,' said Griffin, 'was to think I could do this alone. I need a partner and a hiding place• where I can sleep, eat and rest.'

'Go on,' said Kemp, listening for any kind of movement in the house.

'I've realised that invisibility is only useful for getting away from people and for approaching them. Therefore it's particularly useful for killing. I can walk round an armed man, kill him and escape. And it is killing we must do.'

'Why killing?' asked Kemp.

'The only way to use my invisibility to our advantage is by starting a Reign of Terror•. The Invisible Man must terrify• and dominate• towns like Port Burdock. He must give his orders, and kill everyone who disobeys• and also those who help them.'

## TERROR
What does the Invisible Man want to do?
How can he terrify people?
What terrifies you?

- **disobeys:** doesn't follow orders
- **dominate:** have power over
- **failed:** didn't succeed
- **glanced:** looked quickly
- **hiding place:** safe place to hide
- **Reign of Terror:** control of a large number of people using fear
- **terrify:** scare

Kemp was listening to the sound of his front door opening and closing.

'But your partner would be in a difficult position,' said Kemp.

'Nobody would know he was a partner,' said Griffin. And then suddenly, 'Sh! What's that downstairs?'

'Nothing,' said Kemp, suddenly beginning to speak loud and fast. 'I don't agree with this, Griffin. Why do you want to play a game against humanity•? How can you hope to find happiness? Don't do it. Instead, publish your results and…'

Griffin interrupted him 'Somebody's downstairs,' he whispered•.

'You're imagining it,' said Kemp.

'Let me see,' said Griffin, and moved towards the door.

And then things happened very quickly. Kemp moved to stop Griffin. Griffin was surprised for a second, and cried, 'Traitor•!' Suddenly the dressing gown opened. Kemp ran out of the room and slammed the door. He tried to lock it but the key fell on the floor. Then he tried to hold the door shut but Griffin managed to open it. Invisible fingers gripped Kemp's throat and he let go of the door handle to defend himself. Griffin pushed the door wide open and Kemp fell on the floor.

Colonel Adye, the recipient• of Kemp's letter, was the chief of the Port Burdock police. He was halfway up the stairs when Kemp suddenly appeared, fighting against a door and falling over. Adye was struck violently — by nothing — and fell down the stairs. He heard the two police officers in the hall shout and run. The front door slammed violently.

Kemp staggered down the stairs, dishevelled and with his lip bleeding. 'He's gone! God help us!' he cried.

---

- **humanity:** human beings in general
- **recipient:** person who received
- **traitor:** someone who betrays someone else
- **whispered:** said very quietly

# 16 THE HUNTING• OF THE INVISIBLE MAN

'He's mad,' said Kemp. 'Inhuman• and completely selfish. He only thinks of himself. He has injured• people and he'll kill people unless we stop him.'

'We must catch him,' said Adye. 'But how?'

'You must use all your men,' said Kemp. 'Prevent him from leaving this area. Watch all trains and roads and shipping. He wants to get some notebooks that are important to him from a man in your police station. A man called Marvel.'

'I know,' said Adye. 'But the tramp says he hasn't got the books.'

'He thinks the tramp has them. And you must prevent him from eating or sleeping, day and night. Everybody in the area must be on alert•. Lock up all food. People must lock up their houses. The whole area must start hunting for him. Use dogs. They can smell him and he's scared of them.'

'Good,' said Adye. 'What else?'

'After eating, his food shows until his body has digested it. So he has to hide after eating. Keep checking everywhere. And hide all weapons•. He can't carry any weapon for long without revealing himself, but if he's near someone, he can find something and kill them.'

'I'll go and organise everything,' said Adye.

---

- **hunting:** (here) search for
- **inhuman:** without human qualities such as compassion
- **injured:** hurt
- **on alert:** awake and ready for danger
- **weapons:** objects used to hurt people e.g. guns

It was all done with incredible speed. Before two o'clock it was still possible for the Invisible Man to leave the area, but after two it became impossible. All transportation was on high alert. And in the area of twenty miles around Port Burdock, men armed with guns and sticks went out in groups of three or four, with dogs, to search the roads and fields.

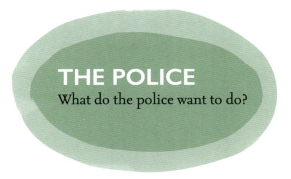

# THE POLICE
### What do the police want to do?

Mounted policemen• rode through the countryside, stopping at every house and warning people to lock their doors and windows. All the schools closed and the children were sent home. But that evening people in the area were horrified by the news of the murder of Mr Wicksteed.

Mr Wicksteed was a quiet man of forty-five or forty-six. The last person to see him alive was a girl walking through a field. She said he looked as if he was trying to reach for something, but she couldn't see what. Madness seemed the only explanation for the murder. The Invisible Man attacked a harmless• man with an iron bar•. He broke his arm and smashed his head to jelly.

- **bar:** long piece of hard metal
- **harmless:** not likely to cause harm
- **mounted policemen:** policemen on horses

# 17 THE SIEGE OF KEMP'S HOUSE

The next day Kemp received the following letter:

> Today is the first day of Terror. Port Burdock is no longer under the Queen. It is under me. This is Day One of Year One of the new age — the Age of the Invisible Man. There will be one execution to set an example — a man named Kemp. Don't help him, my people, or Death will come for you also. Today Kemp will die.

Kemp called his servants and told them to check that all the doors and windows were locked and to close all the shutters. From a drawer in his bedroom he took a small gun and put it in his pocket. He wrote a note to Adye, and gave it to his servant to deliver.

'There's no danger to you,' he said.

'We will catch him!' he thought. 'And I am the bait.'

Suddenly he heard the front doorbell. It was Adye.

'The Invisible Man has attacked your servant!' he said. 'A note from you was snatched out of her hand. He's near here. What was the note about?'

Kemp gave Adye the Invisible Man's letter.

'I suggested setting a trap in my note,' said Kemp. 'But like a fool, I sent the note out with my servant.'

- **bait:** (here) something intended to attract someone to catch them
- **execution:** the act of killing someone as punishment
- **new age:** beginning of a new period of time
- **setting a trap:** plan a situation to catch someone

- **shutters:**
- **siege:** situation when a building is surrounded until the people inside surrender
- **snatched:** taken with force

There was a loud noise of smashing glass from upstairs.

'It's a window!' shouted Kemp. Another smashing sound followed.

'He's going to do the whole house,' said Kemp. 'But he's a fool. The shutters are up and the glass will fall outside. He'll cut his feet.'

'Have you got a gun?' asked Adye.

'Yes, but only one. It has five bullets in it.'

'Give it to me. I'll go to the police station and get the dogs. I'll bring it back,' said Adye. 'You'll be safe here.'

Kemp gave him the gun and went to the door. He unlocked it as silently as possible. Adye went out quickly and was near the gate when a Voice said, 'Stop!'

Adye stopped.

'Where are you going?' said the Voice.

'Where I go,' Adye said slowly, 'is my own business.' The words were still on his lips when he was hit and fell backwards. He drew his gun and fired, but the weapon was taken from his hand.

The Voice laughed. Adye saw the gun in mid-air above him.

'Get up,' said the Voice. 'Don't try any games and go back to the house.'

Kemp was in his study, crouching• among the broken glass and peering• over the edge of the window sill•. He saw Adye talking. 'Why doesn't he fire?' he thought. Then the gun moved a little, and Kemp realised that the Invisible Man was holding it.

---

- **crouching:** putting his body in a low defensive position
- **peering:** looking with difficultly
- **window sill:** shelf below a window

Adye turned and walked towards the house, with the gun following him. Then things happened very quickly. Adye turned around. He tried to grab the gun and missed• it. Then he threw up his hands and fell forward on his face, leaving smoke in the air. Kemp did not hear the shot.

There was a loud knocking at the front door. Kemp armed himself with a poker and went to check that all the windows on the ground floor were locked. Everything was safe and quiet. He returned to his study. Adye lay in the garden, but Kemp saw his servant and two policemen coming towards the house.

Suddenly he heard heavy blows and the sound of wood breaking. Kemp followed the noise and opened the kitchen door just as the broken shutters came flying into the kitchen. 'He's found the axe•!' he thought. And then he saw the gun pointing at him through the broken shutter. He moved back, and the Invisible Man fired a shot but missed him.

Kemp slammed and locked the door. Griffin shouted and laughed, and the axe started again. 'He'll be inside any moment now,' he thought. 'This door won't keep him out for long.'

The front doorbell rang again. It was his servant and the two policemen. Kemp quickly let them in and locked the door again.

'The Invisible Man!' said Kemp. 'He has a gun with two shots left. He's in the kitchen — or will be soon. He's found an axe. And he's killed Adye.'

## ADYE

Why does he leave the house?
How many shots does he fire?
What happens to him?

• **axe:**

• **missed:** didn't hit

Suddenly they heard blows on the kitchen door and then the door opening.

'This way,' said Kemp, and led the men into the dining room.

Kemp handed the dining-room poker to one policeman and the one he was carrying to the other. The axe and the gun appeared.

The gun fired its penultimate• shot and tore• a painting. One of the policemen hit the gun with his poker and sent it to the floor. The axe hit him on the head and he fell, but fortunately he was wearing a helmet. The second policeman, aiming behind the axe, hit something soft that snapped•. There was a cry of pain and the axe fell to the ground. The policeman put his foot on the axe and struck again. Then he stood holding the poker, listening.

He heard the dining-room window open and the sound of running feet. The first policeman sat up, with blood running down between his eye and ear.

'Where is he?'

'Don't know. I've hit him. He may still be here.'

Suddenly they heard the sound of bare feet on the kitchen floor.

'He's escaped through the back door!' said the first policeman.

They went into the dining room.

'Doctor Kemp…' one of the policeman began and then stopped.

The dining-room window was wide open, and there was no sign of Dr Kemp.

## WEAPONS

What weapons does the Invisible Man use?
How does he get them?
What does he do with them?

• **penultimate:** one before the last one    • **tore:** put a hole in
• **snapped:** broke suddenly

# 18 THE HUNTER HUNTED

Kemp ran towards the town. The road was deserted and the distance seemed endless. He could hear the sound of footsteps behind him. He was terrified.

As he entered the town, he could see heaps of gravel• by the road. He passed the door of the Jolly Cricketers and saw a tram driver staring at him and the astonished faces of road workers peering above the gravel.

'The Invisible Man!' he cried to the workers, pointing vaguely behind him. Then he turned into a little side street, then turned again. He ran back into the main street, trying to attract as much attention• as he could.

He looked up the street and saw a huge road worker running towards him carrying a spade•, followed by the tram driver and other men. Men and women were running towards him from the other direction too, some carrying sticks. Kemp stopped, breathing heavily.

'He's near here!' he cried. 'Form a line across…'

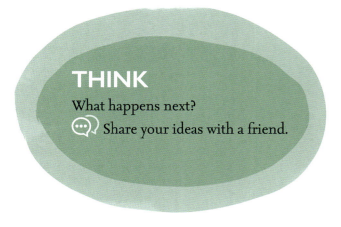

**THINK**

What happens next?

Share your ideas with a friend.

- **attract attention:** make people notice
- **gravel:** lots of very small stones

- **spade:**

Suddenly he was hit hard under the ear. He managed to stay on his feet and he struck a blow that hit nothing. Then he was hit again and fell on the ground. He felt a knee on his stomach. Two hands gripped his throat, one with a weaker grip than the other.

He gripped the wrists and heard a cry of pain. Then the spade of the road worker came down through the air and struck with a thud•. He felt a drop• of something on his face. The grip on his throat suddenly relaxed, and with a huge effort Kemp got on top of the Invisible Man. He gripped the unseen elbows near the ground.

'I've got him!' screamed Kemp. 'Help! He's down! Hold his feet!'

After that, the only sounds were of blows, kicks and heavy breathing.

The Invisible Man tried to fight back, but Kemp didn't let him go. Then suddenly there was a wild scream of 'Mercy•! Mercy!' and a choking• sound.

'Get back,' cried Kemp. 'He's hurt. Stand back!'

People moved away, and Kemp, with his face bruised• and his lips bleeding, seemed to examine the air.

'His mouth's all wet,' he said.

And then, 'Good God! He's not breathing. I can't feel his heart!'

Suddenly an old woman screamed and pointed. And looking where she pointed, everyone saw veins, arteries, bones and tendons and the outline of a transparent hand.

'There are his feet!' cried a policeman.

- **bruised:** with blue skin where it has been hurt
- **choking:** struggling to breathe
- **drop:** (here)

- **mercy:** (here) a cry for compassion instead of harm
- **thud:** heavy sound

Slowly, beginning at his hands and feet, the strange change continued. The tendons appeared, then the bones, veins and arteries, then the flesh and skin. At first the body resembled a mist and then it quickly became dense and opaque•. Now they could see his battered• chest and face.

When at last the crowd moved away for Kemp to stand up, the bruised and broken body of a young man of about thirty lay on the ground. His hair and beard were albino-white, his eyes were wide open and like red glass, and he looked angry and distressed•.

'Cover him!' said a man. 'For God's sake, cover that face!'

Someone brought a sheet and they carried the body into the Jolly Cricketers. It was there that Griffin, the most brilliant physicist the world has ever seen, ended his strange and terrible career.

## KEMP

Imagine you are Kemp.
What would you say about the Invisible Man to a friend?
💬 Talk with a partner.

• **battered:** injured very badly
• **distressed:** very upset and worried

• **opaque:** not transparent

# THE EPILOGUE•

🎧 If you want to learn more about the story, you must go to the Invisible Man, a little inn near Port Burdock. The landlord is a fat man with short arms and legs and a big nose. He will tell you what happened to him after the death of the Invisible Man. The magistrate• tried to take away the money they found on him. But they couldn't prove whose money it was, so they had to give up•.

And if you want to stop his stories, ask him about the three books. He admits he had them, but says that the Invisible Man took them. And then he leaves the bar.

And every night, when the inn is closed, he unlocks a cupboard and then a drawer in the cupboard. He takes out three books, puts them on the table and tries to study them.

'How clever he was!' he thinks. 'When I can understand these, I won't do what he did. I'll just... well...'

Then he goes into a dream, the wonderful dream of his life.

## THE LANDLORD
Who is the landlord?
Who did the money really belong to?
What do you think happens in the landlord's dream?
💬 Talk with a partner.

---

- **epilogue:** part of a book after the end of the main story
- **give up:** stop trying
- **magistrate:** judge

# AFTER READING TALK ABOUT THE STORY

1 **Answer the questions.**
   a Did you enjoy reading the story? Why/Why not?
   b In your opinion, was Griffin interesting as a character? Say why/why not.
   c Do you think H. G. Wells intended the other characters to be interesting? Say why/why not.
   d Do you think there is a hero in this story? If you do, who is it, and why?
   e Which is the best part of the story? Why?
   f Imagine you are Dr Kemp: would you do what he did?
   g Do you think the characters' reactions to Griffin's invisibility are realistic?
   h Do you think Griffin's development is realistic?
   i Would you like to see a film version of The Invisible Man?
   j Imagine you are the director of the film version of the story: which famous actors would you cast as Griffin and Dr Kemp? Why?

2 Share your ideas with the class.

3 Work in small groups. Make a list of films or stories you know in which:
   a a scientific experiment is carried out with no consideration for the consequences.
   b the main character loses control and becomes increasingly dangerous.
   c someone is killed when their dream comes true.

4 Compare your group's lists with the other groups' lists. Did anybody include the same films or stories?

# AFTER READING COMPREHENSION

**1** Read the sentences and tick (✓) T (true) or F (false). Correct the false sentences.

|   |   | T | F |
|---|---|---|---|
| **a** | Iping is an important town that attracts a lot of tourists. | ☐ | ☐ |
| **b** | Griffin becomes part of the community in Iping. | ☐ | ☐ |
| **c** | Griffin has a lot of money. | ☐ | ☐ |
| **d** | It is difficult for people in Iping to trust Griffin. | ☐ | ☐ |
| **e** | Whit Monday is a big community event in Iping. | ☐ | ☐ |
| **f** | Mr Marvel is happy to help Griffin. | ☐ | ☐ |
| **g** | Griffin learns that invisibility has fewer advantages than he thought. | ☐ | ☐ |
| **h** | Griffin cannot carry anything without revealing his presence. | ☐ | ☐ |
| **i** | Griffin wants to use his invisibility to become rich and then become visible again. | ☐ | ☐ |
| **j** | Griffin thinks Kemp will help him because they are both scientists. | ☐ | ☐ |

**2** 💬 Work with a partner and explain the part that the following things play in the story.

**a**  **b**  **c**  **d**

**3** Tick (✓) all the things that can reveal Griffin's presence when he's alive and naked.

| | |
|---|---|
| ☐ snow | ☐ breathing |
| ☐ his shadow | ☐ his hair |
| ☐ rain | ☐ sneezing |
| ☐ fog | ☐ dust |
| ☐ his eyes | ☐ undigested food in his stomach |
| ☐ his strength | ☐ the blood in his veins |
| ☐ dogs | ☐ his footprints |

**4** Read the text and answer the questions. Then share your answers with the class.

A calendar year is 365 days, but the Earth takes 365 ¼ days to revolve around the Sun. So every four years a day is added to the calendar. The extra day, called Leap Day, is February 29th, and the year is called a Leap Year. Hundreds of years ago, the Leap Day was not recognised in British law. As the day had no legal status, people decided they were allowed break from tradition on that day so, for example, it is the day in which women can propose marriage to men. There are many myths about the Leap Year in different countries: it's considered very unlucky in some, very lucky in others, bad for farming, bad for getting married, and some people believe that more people die in a Leap Year than in other years.

**a** The story begins with Griffin's arrival in Iping during a snow storm on February 29th. What is Wells telling us by choosing that date?

**b** Are there any traditions or myths about the Leap Year in your country? If so, what are they?

**c** Do you know anybody who was born on February 29th? If so, when do they celebrate their birthday in non-leap years?

# AFTER READING CHARACTERS

**1  Answer the questions.**

  **a**  Which character is very intelligent, decisive and brave?

  **b**  Which character is the first to be hit by an invisible fist, but is too shocked to tell the others?

  **c**  Which character kills himself?

  **d**  Which characters see some bloody footprints?

  **e**  Which character is the first person to fight Griffin?

  **f**  Whose house does Griffin set on fire?

  **g**  Which character pretends to be Griffin's friend?

  **h**  Who is Griffin's last victim?

  **i**  Which character doesn't trust Griffin from the start?

  **j**  Who has their only companion taken away by Griffin?

  **k**  Which character is robbed and imprisoned in their own house?

  **l**  Who is shot and killed by Griffin?

  **m**  Which two characters investigate Griffin's room at the Coach and Horses?

  **n**  Who benefits from the events in the story?

**2  Answer the questions below. Write about 50 words for each one giving reasons for your answers.**

**GRIFFIN**

**KEMP**

**ADYE**

  **a**  In what ways are Griffin and Kemp similar?

  **b**  In what ways are they different?

  **c**  In what ways are Kemp and Adye similar?

**3  Read the sentences and tick (✓) T (true) or F (false).**

|   |   | T | F |
|---|---|---|---|
| **a** | Adye walks back to the house with a gun following him. | ☐ | ☐ |
| **b** | Mr Bunting goes down the stairs holding an axe. | ☐ | ☐ |
| **c** | Mr Marvel studies Kemp's books secretly. | ☐ | ☐ |
| **d** | The landlord in Great Portland Street doesn't trust Griffin and thinks he's a burglar. | ☐ | ☐ |
| **e** | Mr Huxter is the first person who is tripped up by Griffin when Marvel runs off with the bundle. | ☐ | ☐ |
| **f** | Mr Jaffers tries to arrest the Invisible Man for burglary. | ☐ | ☐ |
| **g** | The American shoots at the Invisible Man to protect Kemp. | ☐ | ☐ |
| **h** | Mr Henfrey notices that the stranger hasn't given his name. | ☐ | ☐ |
| **i** | Kemp finds mud all over his bed. | ☐ | ☐ |
| **j** | At first, Mrs Hall is worried the stranger may be ill. | ☐ | ☐ |

**4  Correct the sentences in Exercise 3 that are false.**

**5  💬 Discuss these questions about Griffin with a partner.**

   **a**  Why did Griffin study light?
   **b**  Why did Griffin make himself invisible?
   **c**  What is Griffin trying to do in Iping?
   **d**  What problems does Griffin have when he is invisible?
   **e**  What kind of help does Griffin want from Mr Marvel?
   **f**  What kind of help does Griffin want from Dr Kemp?
   **g**  Does Griffin change during the story, and if so, in what ways and why?

# AFTER READING VOCABULARY

**1** **Match the words to the definitions. Two words have the same definition.**

**a** ☐ cry        **e** ☐ shout

**b** ☐ whisper      **f** ☐ scream

**c** ☐ muffle       **g** ☐ howl

**d** ☐ rave        **h** ☐ exclaim

**1** to talk in a very angry, uncontrolled way
**2** to say something very loudly
**3** to make a loud, high sound because you are in pain, frightened or angry
**4** to make a long, loud sound like a dog, usually to express pain or sadness
**5** say in a surprised way
**6** to speak very quietly, using the breath but not the voice
**7** to make a quiet, less clear sound

**2** **Complete the sentences with the correct form of the verbs in Exercise 1. There can be more than one answer.**

**a** Mrs Bunting was woken by a noise. She woke her husband and softly ............................ , 'I think there's somebody downstairs.'

**b** He had a hand over his mouth, so his voice was ............................ .

**c** The strange man ............................ for hours about his many problems.

**d** People were so frightened that they ............................ and ran away.

**e** Last night someone was ............................ like a wolf in the fields near Port Burdock.

**f** 'You set the house on fire!' ............................ Kemp.

**g** When Griffin realised what was going on, he looked at Dr Kemp and angrily ............................ , 'Traitor!'

**h** As he ran towards the road workers and the crowd in the street, Dr Kemp ............................ 'The Invisible Man!' so that everybody could hear him.

**3** Circle the word in each group that is different to the others. Explain why to a friend.

| | | | |
|---|---|---|---|
| **a** stranger | traitor | bandage | landlord |
| **b** crouch | tramp | punch | rush |
| **c** poker | injure | axe | spade |
| **d** gagged | exhausted | distressed | irritated |
| **e** yawn | sneeze | shoot | gasp |

**4** Answer the questions using a word in Exercise 3.

**a** What might you do when you're very surprised by something? ........................... .

**b** What might you do if you've got a cold? ........................... .

**c** If you're injured and have a wound, what is usually put on it? ........................... .

**d** What do you use to dig in the ground? ........................... .

**e** What might you do if you're exhausted? ........................... .

**f** What might you do if a stranger attacks you in the street? ........................... .

**g** If someone betrays their country, what are they? ........................... .

**5** Look at the pictures below. Write your own definitions for the objects.

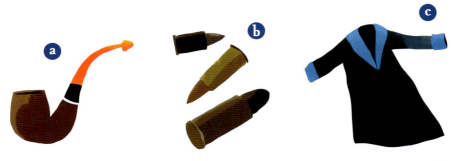

85

# AFTER READING LANGUAGE

**1** **Rewrite the following sentences using the words given and the active form.**

   **a**  All his head above his blue goggles was covered by a white bandage. (A white bandage)

   **b**  Mr Hall was struck violently in the chest and thrown out of the room. (Somebody)

   **c**  The door was slammed in Mr Hall's face and locked. (Somebody)

   **d**  Griffin's books weren't understood by anyone. (No one)

   **e**  Once or twice things were broken with sudden violence. (Once or twice the stranger)

   **f**  A match was struck and the study was filled with yellow light. (Somebody/yellow light)

   **g**  Suddenly he was hit hard under the ear. (Somebody)

   **h**  Marvel was suddenly taken by the neck and shaken violently. (The Invisible Man)

**2** **Rewrite the following sentences using the passive form. Use 'by' only when necessary.**

   **a**  The shirt-sleeve punched Mr Hall's face.

   **b**  Two shop assistants chased Griffin around the store.

   **c**  Did people search the roads and fields all day?

   **d**  A blow suddenly shook the door.

   **e**  The Invisible Man tripped up three men and they fell on the ground.

   **f**  Someone struck him violently in the chest.

   **g**  How many people did Griffin attack and kill?

   **h**  The servant didn't deliver Kemp's note to Colonel Adye.

**3** 💬 **Work with a partner. Explain the difference in meaning between these two sentences. Which is the first conditional? Which is the second conditional?**

**a** If the Invisible Man finds Marvel, the tramp will be terrified.

**b** If the Invisible Man found Marvel, the tramp would be terrified.

**4** **Read the situations. Decide how likely they are to happen. Then write sentences using either the first or second conditional.**

a  You find $500,000 under your bed.
   If I ............................................................................................................ .
b  You eat too much tomorrow.
c  Your best friend rings you this evening.
d  You wake up and find you are a monkey.
e  There's a big fire in the building next door.
f  You go to bed late at the weekend.

**5** **Read these sentences. Underline the relative pronouns and circle the words they refer to.**

a  The only light in the room was from the fire, which lit his goggles but left the rest of his face in darkness.
b  He had an enormous mouth that filled the lower half of his face.
c  They heard the sound of rustling paper again — it was the savings that the vicar kept in the drawer.
d  A stranger in a large hat that hid his face walked in.
e  The man who stood there shouting an incomprehensible explanation had no head.
f  'I'll show him,' shouted the American, and shot five bullets in the direction which the stones were coming from.
g  'It's all in the books that the tramp has stolen.'

# AFTER READING PLOT AND THEME

**1** **Put Griffin's actions in the order in which he did them. Write the letters in the first row of boxes.**

|      | 1 | 2 | 3 | 4 | 5 | 6 | 7 | 8 | 9 | 10 | 11 | 12 | 13 |
|------|---|---|---|---|---|---|---|---|---|----|----|----|----|
| Ex 1 |   |   |   |   |   |   |   |   |   |    |    |    |    |
| Ex 2 |   |   |   |   |   |   |   |   |   |    |    |    |    |

    **a**  Robbed the shopkeeper and left him tied and gagged in his house.
    **b**  Discovered a formula for invisibility.
    **c**  Attacked Kemp's house and killed Colonel Adye.
    **d**  Tried to kill Marvel.
    **e**  Made himself invisible.
    **f**  Took the old woman's cat and experimented with it.
    **g**  Took up physics to study light.
    **h**  Murdered Mr Wicksteed.
    **i**  Robbed his father and didn't feel guilty about it.
    **j**  Set the lodging house on fire.
    **k**  Chased Kemp and tried to kill him.
    **l**  Robbed Iping's vicar.
    **m** Forced Marvel to help him.

**2** **Now put Griffin's actions on the order in which they are told in the story. Write the letters in the second row of boxes.**

**3** **Look at the numbers for each action and answer the questions.**
    **a**  Are they the same for each action?
    **b**  Did the author tell the story in chronological order?
    **c**  What did the author do?
    **d**  What is the effect of the author's choice?

**4** **Read the text and answer the questions.**

> H. G. Wells believed that a science fiction story should contain only one single 'magic', fantastic and extraordinary element. He wrote that, 'As soon as the magic trick has been done, the whole business of the fantasy writer is to keep everything else human and real.'

  **a** Which extraordinary element or elements are in *The Invisible Man*?
  **b** Is everything else in the story human and real? If not, what is not realistic?
  **c** Can you give two examples of something human and real in the story?
  **d** Did H. G. Wells follow his own rules in *The Invisible Man*? If not, in what ways did he break them?

**5** **What are the themes of the story? Read the sentences and tick (✓) the ones that apply.**

  **a** ☐ Scientists must always think about the consequences of their work and actions.
  **b** ☐ People may use science for evil purposes.
  **c** ☐ It is important to believe in yourself.
  **d** ☐ Scientific advances can have bad results as well as good results.
  **e** ☐ Society is changing fast.
  **f** ☐ It is possible for society to lose control of its scientific and technological achievements.
  **g** ☐ Scientists must not try to gain a personal advantage from their discoveries.
  **h** ☐ Society should be able to say yes or no to new technology.

**6** 💬 **Discuss your answers to Exercise 5 with a partner. Which themes do you most agree with? Why?**

# TECHNOLOGY

## THE LUDDITE REBELLION•

Today, the word Luddite is generally used to mean someone who is too old-fashioned to like and use technological innovations. However, the origins of the word mark the beginning of a conflict• that started with the Industrial Revolution• and continues today. The Luddites were a social movement• which started in the British Midlands in 1811. The name comes from a probably fictional story about a young worker called Ned Ludd, who smashed a textile• machine. The Luddites were skilled textile workers who, during the Industrial Revolution, found themselves unable to earn a living and feed their families. This was because industrialists and factory owners were replacing the skilled workers with machines that could be operated by cheap unskilled workers. The result was that skilled workers became unemployed and unskilled workers worked long hours for very low pay, while the industrialists became increasingly rich. The Luddites organised protests and often smashed the machines. In fact, they weren't against the machines. They wanted better pay and skilled workers to work the machines. Their movement was so strong and so many people supported them that the army was sent to stop the rebellion.

After a trial in the city of York in 1813, seventeen men were executed•.

LIFE SKILLS

# AT WORK

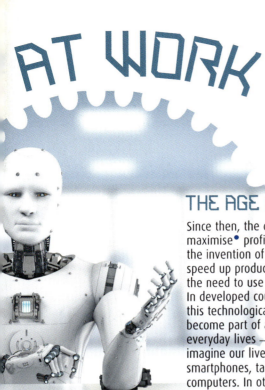

Look at your answers to Exercise 5 on page 89. Are any of the themes relevant to the Luddites' rebellion? Are any of the themes relevant to the automation of today's jobs?

## THE AGE OF ROBOTS

Since then, the desire to maximise• profits has encouraged the invention of technologies that speed up production and reduce the need to use people to do work. In developed countries, some of this technological innovation has become part of a lot of people's everyday lives — most of us cannot imagine our lives without our smartphones, tablets and home computers. In other words, society has accepted these things by buying them. However, the digital revolution is also having other effects. As more and more jobs are done by robots, fewer and fewer people are needed to operate the machines. And the jobs that are taken by robots are not being replaced by other "human" jobs. In other words, there are fewer jobs in general. Now, in the twenty-first century, we are entering a new phase of automation•. Driverless cars, robots and delivery drones are increasingly replacing people in the transport and distribution industries. Will workers protest against automation as they have done in the past?
Or will new technology bring more advantages than disadvantages?

**Luddite**

/ˈlʌdaɪt/ noun [C] a person who is opposed to new technology or ways of working

- **automation:** when things are run by machines, not people
- **conflict:** fight
- **executed:** killed as a punishment
- **Industrial Revolution:** period of time when machines, steam power and factories were developed
- **maximise:** make as large as possible
- **movement:** group of people working together to make their shared ideas happen
- **rebellion:** situation when people fight authority or the normal way of doing something
- **textile:** material

**P** **B2 Preliminary English Test Reading Part 1**

1  **A group of friends are organising a fancy-dress party on the theme of The Invisible Man. Read each text: What does it say? Tick (✓) the correct answer.**

**a**

> Jane, there's a rumour that five different people want to bring a white cat — is it true? It could be messy, especially if the cats don't get along. I think we should discourage the idea. Billy.

1  ☐  Five people are bringing a white cat.

2  ☐  Billy wants to tell people that bringing a cat is not a good idea.

3  ☐  Jane has a cat that doesn't get along with other cats.

**b**

You won't believe this — I've found pink contact lenses! I already have the wig, the beard, and the white face cream, so my costume is ready! 👍 Paul

1  ☐  Paul wants to go as Marvel.

2  ☐  Paul wants to go as the landlord.

3  ☐  Paul wants to go as Griffin.

**c**

I think we should have a competition. Of all those that come as The Wrapped-Up Stranger, the one who keeps the full costume on the longest wins a prize (not yet decided). Amy

1  ☐  The Wrapped-Up Stranger fancy dress will be the longest.

2  ☐  The Wrapped-Up Stranger fancy dress will be uncomfortable.

3  ☐  Amy wants to decide on a prize.

**d**

→ Abc ✉ ⊘ Send

> Girls, we don't all have to come as Mrs Hall, The Poor Woman From Downstairs or Kemp's Servant — we can dress up as a male character if we want! Sally

1. ☐ Sally wants to go as a male character.
2. ☐ The girls shouldn't go as female characters.
3. ☐ Girls should feel free to go as a female or as a male character.

**e**

ATTENTION! To all those planning to come as Marvel: we all know that he must be very smelly, but please be kind to the rest of us and omit that part of the costume! 😂
Jenny

1. ☐ People going as Marvel should look dirty but not smell.
2. ☐ Jenny hopes nobody will go as Marvel.
3. ☐ There is one part of Marvel's costume that people must not wear.

**f**

→ Abc ✉ ⊘ Send

> Hey guys, no fake blood please. Let's avoid staining the carpet by using our imaginations a little.
> Jack

1. ☐ Jack's carpet is stained.
2. ☐ Jack doesn't want the carpet to be stained.
3. ☐ Jack is bringing fake blood.

1 ▶ MP3 **Listen and tick (✓) the correct picture.**

a 1 ☐     2 ☐

b 1 ☐     2 ☐

c 1 ☐     2 ☐

d 1 ☐     2 ☐

## 2 P Read the text and choose the correct words 1, 2, 3 or 4.

*The Invisible Man* is the story of a brilliant scientist, Griffin, who is
**a** .............. by light and discovers a **b** .............. for invisibility. After
more than three years of **c** .............. he succeeds in making himself
invisible. Griffin believes that invisibility will give him great power.
**d** .............., he only knows how to make himself invisible, but not how
to reverse the process. To his great surprise, he discovers that being
invisible does not give him the **e** .............. he dreamt of and
**f** .............. there are very few things it is useful for. As time goes by
and his **g** .............. grows, he becomes more and more **h** ..............
and violent. When he finds Dr Kemp, he has decided to start a 'Reign
of Terror' to get what he wants, and Dr Kemp informs the police. The
police **i** .............. Griffin and find him but by that time he has already
**j** .............. two people.

| | | | | |
|---|---|---|---|---|
| **a** | **1** astonished | **2** fascinated | **3** interested | **4** attracted |
| **b** | **1** invention | **2** way | **3** formula | **4** method |
| **c** | **1** experiences | **2** exams | **3** projects | **4** experiments |
| **d** | **1** However | **2** Although | **3** Unless | **4** So |
| **e** | **1** advantages | **2** hopes | **3** fame | **4** career |
| **f** | **1** that | **2** which | **3** then | **4** too |
| **g** | **1** emotion | **2** horror | **3** exhaustion | **4** exasperation |
| **h** | **1** jealous | **2** invisible | **3** aggressive | **4** transparent |
| **i** | **1** hunt | **2** follow | **3** search | **4** see |
| **j** | **1** destroyed | **2** damaged | **3** murdered | **4** smashed |

# AFTER READING PROJECT

**Work in small groups. Make a poster or a video about a scientific experiment, real or fictional, that had a terrible result, and present it to the class. Find images and include answers to these questions:**

- Is the experiment real or fictional?
- Where and when did this happen?
- Was the experiment carried out by one scientist or by a team?
- Who did the scientist(s) work for?
- What was the purpose of the experiment?
- Was the experiment successful?
- In what way were the results terrible?
- Was there anything positive about the experiment?
- Did innocent people die?
- Did any of the scientists regret doing their research?
- What happened to the scientists?
- Are there any similarities between this experiment and *The Invisible Man*?